Parables of Jesus
The Mustard Seed and Other Stories

WRITTEN AND ILLUSTRATED BY
Helen Caswell

Abingdon Press

Nashville

Parables of Jesus
The Mustard Seed and Other Stories

ISBN 0-687-05606-3

98 99 00 01 02 03 04 05 06 07 — 10 9 8 7 6 5 4 3 2 1

Manufactured in Hong Kong

Contents

Parable of the Mustard Seed

READ MATTHEW 13:31-32

*I*n my hand I have a mustard seed.

*I*t is so tiny that you can hardly see it.

I plant my mustard seed in a pot.

I put it in a sunny place.

I give it some water, and soon it begins to grow.

*E*very day it grows a little bit more.

$\mathcal{W}$eeks go by . . . and it is a BIG plant.

*I*n the meadow are many more plants, all from tiny seeds.

*F*aith in God is like a mustard seed.

You can't see it, but it is very important.

$\mathcal{L}$ike the tiny seeds, faith is full of life and beauty.

Parable of the Lost Sheep

READ MATTHEW 18:10-14

*H*ere is a shepherd.

$\mathcal{H}$e has many, many sheep to look after.

*E*ven though there are so many sheep,
he knows each one by name.

One silly little sheep named Bluebell
is always wandering off.

One day Bluebell is missing.

The shepherd looks everywhere for Bluebell. He is afraid she might have fallen in the water.

*O*r she might have gone into the mountains.

*F*inally the shepherd finds her,
caught in some brambles.

The shepherd is so happy to find his lost sheep that he doesn't even scold her.

Everyone is happy to see Bluebell,
even though she is so silly.

*J*esus says that God is like the shepherd.
Even though there are so many people,
God loves every one of us,
and he is especially happy when someone
who has wandered away
comes back.

Parable of
the Lost Coin

READ LUKE 15:8-10

Maria worked at painting designs on pots made of clay.

One day she took her pots to market, so that people could buy them.

$\mathcal{M}$aria sold so many pots that
she had ten coins for her very own.

As soon as she got home,
Maria counted her coins into a pile.
She was very pleased with them.

But when she started to put them away,
one was missing!
There were only nine coins!

Maria was very upset.
She began hunting everywhere
for her lost coin.
First she swept the whole house, very carefully,
in case the coin had dropped onto the floor
and rolled into a corner.

*T*hen she shook out all the bedding
(and aired it), in case the coin
had slipped down under
a blanket.

And although she didn't know
how a coin could have jumped on top
of the tall cupboard,
she looked there, too (and dusted,
while she was at it).

She even weeded the little garden in the dooryard, because the coin *might* be among the flowers.

And then, finally, she found it—
in a crack between the floorboards.
Why hadn't she seen it before?

No matter. She had found it, and she was so happy (and the house was so clean) that she had a party and invited all her friends to help her celebrate.
Jesus says that God and the angels celebrate,
just as Maria did, when someone who
has been lost comes back to God.

Parable of
the Leaven

READ MATTHEW 13:33

At the store we buy a great big bag of flour
and a little tiny package of yeast,
which is also called "leaven."

*A*t home in the kitchen we get ready to bake.

*I*n a big bowl we mix a spoonful of yeast with some warm milk, and then we put in lots and lots of flour.

*A*nd we let it rise.
The yeast makes it swell up
twice as big as when we started.

*T*hen we knead it and make it into loaves of bread.

*A*nd cinnamon rolls.

*A*nd all sorts of good things.

*W*e wait until the yeast
makes them swell up twice as big again.

*T*hen we put them in the oven and bake them.

*T*hey come out warm and delicious
and light as a feather.
The yeast has worked like magic!

The Kingdom of God is like the yeast, Jesus said.
If we mixed the flour and milk without yeast,
It would turn out as hard as rocks.
The yeast makes it full of life and lightness,
and lots bigger than when it started!